Contents

In the Beginning

S pace is all around us and scientists think that it stretches on forever. As you'd expect, something that big has a lot of things in it. Let's find out what's there.

SOLAR SYSTEM

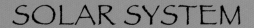

Our *solar system* has the Sun at its centre. Eight planets and lots of comets and other space rocks constantly circle around it.

WHAT'S THAT NOISE?

Between 10-15 billion years ago, the universe exploded and the world was created. This is called the Big Bang theory.

Scientists believe that the centre of the Sun is 15,000,000° C!

MOON

A planet is an object over a certain size that *orbits* a star. Planets are made of three things: rock, ice or gas. A moon is an object over a certain size that orbits around a planet rather than a star—just like our Moon.

5

SHINING STAR

Stars are really just big balls of gas. They come in all sizes and temperatures. Our Sun is just one of billions of stars. It looks different from all the other stars because we're very close to it.

THE SMALL ONES

Asteroids are rocks that orbit stars but are too small to be called planets. Comets are similar, but are made of ice and dust. Meteors are lumps of rock and iron that fall to earth and can sometimes be seen blazing across the sky.

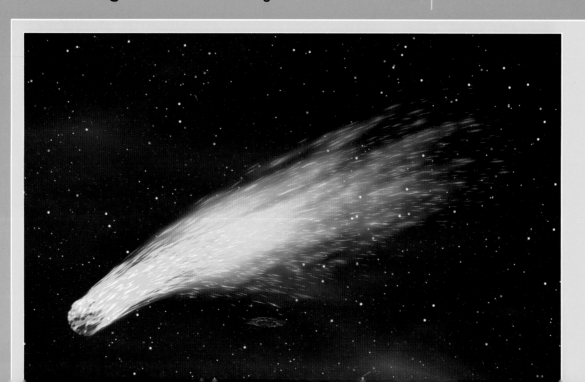

Star Light, Star Bright

S tars are not just dots of light that look pretty— there's more going on up there than you might think.

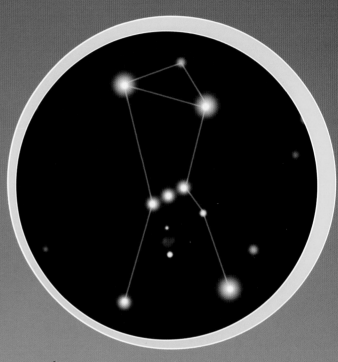

MAKING PICTURES

Constellations are imaginary lines drawn between stars to form pictures. There are 88 different constellations that help people to *navigate*.

GANGING UP

Stars belong to groups called *galaxies*. Our own galaxy is called the Milky Way and contains up to 400 billion stars.

7

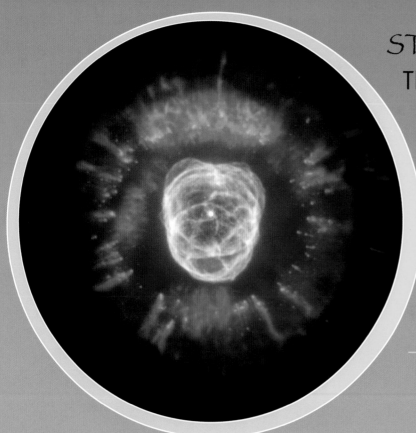

STAR FACTORIES

There are huge clouds of gas and dust in space called nebulae. When gas and dust spin quickly out of a nebula, a star is born. You can sometimes see this through a telescope if you're lucky.

Galaxies come in three shapes: spiral, elliptical (oval-shaped) and irregular.

SUPERNOVAS

Stars sometimes end in a huge explosion called a supernova! Luckily, our Sun isn't expected to die for another five billion years.

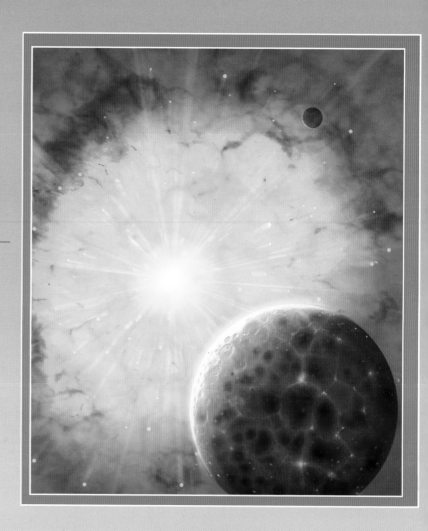

Eyes on the Skies

F rom the very start of time, people have found the stars fascinating. As technology has improved, we have learnt more than ever before.

LOOKING HARD

Astronomers use telescopes to watch space. They are used in special buildings called observatories. These are usually high up in hills or mountains so that pollution and cloud can't get in the way.

FIRST GLANCE

The first telescope was invented in the 1600s. This was when people could see the craters on the Moon for the first time.

HUBBLE BUBBLE

In 1990 the Hubble Telescope was launched into space. It is so close to the stars and planets that it sends back amazingly clear pictures. It has even photographed stars being born.

Astronomers point lots of small telescopes at the same area of sky instead of using one big one.

HEAR! HEAR!

Objects such as stars give off radio waves. Radio telescopes such as the Arecibo telescope in Puerto Rico can pick up these waves.

Infinity and Beyond

S cientists use spacecrafts to get up close to things they want to study. The crafts all do different jobs once they're up in space.

THE FIRST

The first *satellite* was launched in 1957 and was very basic. Now satellites can do many jobs, such as weather forecasting. There are over 2500 orbiting in space right now!

A CLOSER LOOK

Probes are sent to look at objects in space for the first time. Some probes are specially designed to crash into objects. This is called a "hard landing".

OFF FOR GOOD

Some probes don't land anywhere. They are sent off into space for as long as their batteries will last. Voyager 1 was launched in 1977. It has travelled about 15 billion miles so far.

There are over 8,000 man-made objects floating around in space—including things astronauts have dropped!

WHEELY USEFUL

Some probes carry rovers with them. These are remote-controlled vehicles designed to drive around the surface of planets. There are two rovers currently exploring Mars.

To Boldly Go

The first person in space was a Russian cosmonaut called Yuri Gagarin, in 1961. This was the start of our space adventure.

BLAST OFF!

Spacecrafts need lots of speed to beat Earth's *gravity* and get into space. The only way to get that kind of speed is to use rockets. The biggest rocket so far is the Saturn V, which was 110 metres high and travelled at over 8600 km per hour!

MOONWALK

Apollo 11 landed on the Moon on July 20th, 1969. Neil Armstrong was the first man to walk on its surface. He famously said that it was "one small step for man, one giant leap for mankind".

RECORD BREAKERS

The first British person in space was Helen Sharman. She travelled with the Russian space program. Russian astronauts are called cosmonauts.

14

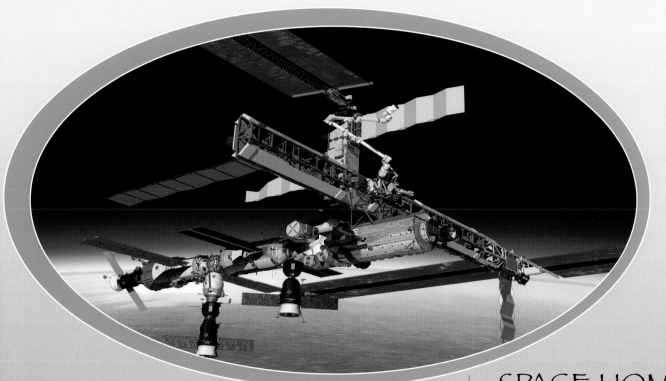

SPACE HOME

Getting people into space costs a lot of money, so astronauts live on the International Space Station for months at a time. It is run by sixteen different countries.

RECYCLING

Each space shuttle mission costs around £222 million! The space shuttle is the world's most complicated machine and is the only reusable spacecraft ever made.

15

One of the space shuttle's jobs is to take scientists and supplies to the International Space Station.

TOOLS AT THE READY

Astronauts have to maintain the space station to keep everything running. They go outside on spacewalks to do repairs. They have to be careful not to drop any equipment, as any space junk that drifts off could damage other missions.

Mysterious Space

Space is big and far away, which means that there are lots of things in it that scientists still don't know about. Here are some of the big mysteries.

WHIRLPOOL

Black holes are tighly packed parts of space which suck in objects around them like a whirlpool. Everything pulled into a black hole is destroyed.

DOCTOR WHO?

Scientists think there may be tunnels in space that lead to different parts of the universe. People could travel through these "wormholes" and pop out somewhere else—even back in time!

17

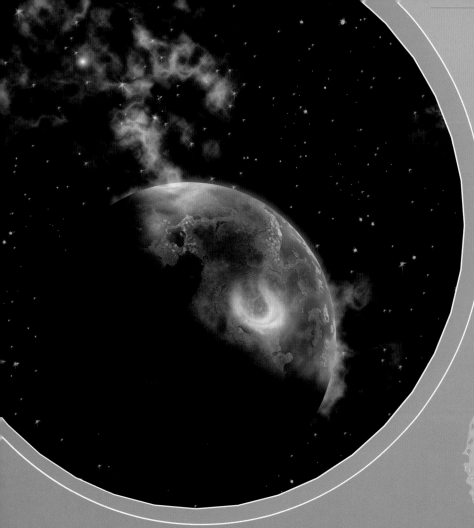

SOMETHING MISSING

Scientists think that over 80 per cent of space has something in it that they can't identify. They call this "dark matter".

Some probes have drawings of humans on them in case any aliens see them.

WE COME IN PEACE

Are we alone in the universe? Many scientists believe that there are living creatures on other planets, including Mars.

Future Space

O ur achievements in space travel are still only the tip of the iceberg. There's lots left to do and explore.

BIG SLEEP

The long distances involved in space travel are a big problem. Journeys could last many years. Scientists are working on a way to stop humans ageing so quickly, called "suspended animation".

HOLIDAY

In 2001 Dennis Tito became the world's first space tourist. He paid to fly in a Russian rocket for a price of £10 million!

BACK TO THE MOON

Since 1969, only 12 people have been to the Moon. However, there are now plans to build a base on the Moon. It would be used as a launch pad for other space missions to far away planets.

A light year is a distance of 10 trillion km!

OFF TO MARS?

A new worldwide race is beginning to send a person to Mars. First of all, probes need find out about conditions on the planet to make sure it's safe.

Victor Habbick

DIZZY HEIGHTS

NASA is planning to build a huge 40,000 km-high elevator reaching from Earth into space. People would be transported into space by trams running on strong cables. You'll have to wait until the end of this century to try it out, though.

AFTER HUBBLE

The Next Generation Space Telescope will be the follow-up to Hubble. It will use a huge mirror to study the formation of stars and to discover the history of the universe.

21

Glossary

ASTRONOMER
Someone who studies the universe and objects which exist in space.

GALAXY
A very large group of stars in the universe.

GRAVITY
The force which pulls things to the ground.

NAVIGATE
To direct the route of a ship or other vehicle using instruments or maps.

ORBIT
To follow a curved path around a planet or star.

PROBE
A small spacecraft sent into space to send back information to scientists on Earth.

SATELLITE
An object moving round a larger object in space.

SOLAR SYSTEM
The sun and the eight planets which move around it, including Earth.

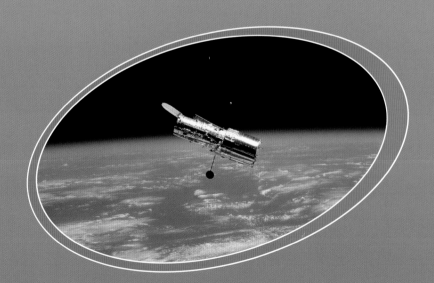

Further Reading

Living on Other Worlds (Our Universe)
Gregory L. Vogt, Raintree Publishers, 2003

Moon Landing (Speedy Reads)
Nick Arnold, Scholastic, 2001

Oxford First Book of Space (Oxford First Series)
Andrew Langley, Oxford University Press, 2003

Space (Kingfisher Voyages)
Mike Goldsmith, Kingfisher Books Ltd, 2006

The Usborne First Encyclopedia of Space
Paul Dowswell, Usborne Publishing Ltd, 2001

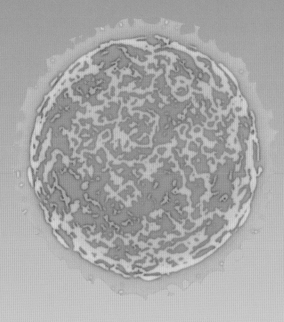

Index

24

UP CLOSE

SPACE

PAUL HARRISON

W
FRANKLIN WATTS
LONDON • SYDNEY

Published in 2008 by Franklin Watts
Reprinted in 2010

Copyright © 2008 Arcturus Publishing Limited

Franklin Watts
338 Euston Road
London NW1 3BH

Franklin Watts Australia
Level 17/207 Kent Street
Sydney NSW 2000

Author: Paul Harrison
Designer (new edition): Silvie Rabbe
Editor (new edition): Fiona Tulloch

Picture credits: Corbis: page 3, bottom right; page 6, bottom; page 9, bottom; page 10, top right; page 11, bottom; page 14; NASA: page 3, top; page 5, top right; page 7, top right; Science Photo Library: page 4, top right; page 5, bottom left; page 6, top right; page 8, top and bottom; page 9, top right; page 10, bottom left; page 15, top and bottom.

A CIP catalogue record for this book is available from the British Library

Dewey number: 520

ISBN: 978-1-4451-0133-0
SL000948EN

Printed in China

Franklin Watts is a division of Hachette Children's Books, an Hachette UK Company
www.hachette.co.uk